CAN YOU SEE WHAT I SEE?
GAMES
READ-AND-SEEK LEVEL 1

WALTER WICK

Cartwheel BOOKS® SCHOLASTIC INC.

New York Toronto London Auckland Sydney
Mexico City New Delhi Hong Kong Buenos Aires

Text copyright © 2007 by Walter Wick.
"Domino Effect," "Card Tricks," "In Bins," "String Game," "Magic Mirror," "Picture Blocks," "Spare Parts," and "Wood Shop" from *Can You See What I See?* © 2002 by Walter Wick; "Games Galore" from *Can You See What I See? Cool Collections* © 2004 by Walter Wick.

All rights reserved. Published by Scholastic Inc.
SCHOLASTIC, CARTWHEEL BOOKS, and associated logos
are trademarks and/or registered trademarks of Scholastic Inc.

Library of Congress Cataloging-in-Publication Data
Wick, Walter.
Can you see what I see? Games read-and-seek / Walter Wick.
p. cm. – (Scholastic reader. Level 1)
ISBN 0-439-86229-9
1. Picture puzzles--Juvenile literature. I. Title. II. Title: Games read-and-seek.
GV1507.P47W5132 2007
793.73–dc22   2006101859

ISBN-13: 978-0-439-86229-5
ISBN-10: 0-439-86229-9

10 9 8 7 6 5 4 3 2 1   7 8 9 10 11/0

Printed in the U.S.A. • First printing, May 2007

Dear Reader,

Read the words and find the hidden objects. For an extra challenge, cover the picture clues at the bottom of each page with your hand.

Have fun!

Walter Wick

Walter Wick

Can you see

a penguin,

a seal,

and a star?

Can you see

a clock,

a key,

and a car?

Can you see

a turtle,

a boat,

and 2 hats?

Can you see

2 helmets,

a baseball,

3 bats?

Can you see

a jack,

a spider,

a spring?

Can you see

2 tops,

and a king

in a sling?

Can you see

a domino,

a ball,

and a frog?

Can you see

an elephant,

a cat,

and a dog?

Can you see

a football,

a golf ball,

a bear?

Can you see

a cat

that is under

a chair?

Can you see

3 squirrels,

8 leaves

that are green?

Can you see

3 boats,

a phone,

and a queen?

ball

baseball

bat

bat

bear

boat

car

cat

clock

dog

domino

elephant

football

frog

golf ball

hat

helmet

jack

key

king

leaves

penguin

phone

queen

seal

spider

spring

squirrel

star

top

turtle